INTRODUCTION: We all know that asking for help isn't always easy, yet, all of us need some help in life. "HELP!" is a 30 day devotional with scriptures and prayers designed to teach and inspire you to ask God for help in all things. We all struggle at times, and unconsciously thinking to yourself, "I could probably use a little help", spends mental and emotional energy without bringing any results. Why? Because needing help and asking for help are two different things. Many of our internal struggles, remain internal. One thing's for sure, if you're human, you need help. Jump into this 30 day devotional and expect to learn new perspectives on receiving help from God. James 4:2-3 tells us that we have not because we ask not, and when we do ask, we ask with wrong motives. God, help us, something has to change. Study this booklet and never forget, Psalm 121:2 MY HELP COMES FROM THE LORD, WHO MADE HEAVEN AND EARTH. Help is on the way!

HELP!

Psalms 121:2 NKJV
"My help comes from the Lord, Who made heaven and earth."

DAY 1

ARE YOU WILLING?

One of the most important attributes that we can exude in our faith in The Lord Jesus Christ, is our willingness to receive help from God.

Why is the willingness to receive help from God important? Because all Help is not created equal, and the beautiful reality that God has given all of us a "free will" comes with a very ugly side. That ugly side brings harm when we use our "free will" to reject, refuse, run away from, neglect, side against, or even despise the loving assistance God has made available to His children, you and me.

People often overlook the treasure of God's help for two common reasons:

1. It's usually simple, not complicated, a child can understand it.
2. It always requires something from us in the form of action and accountability.

Remember Adam and Eve?
Somehow, the importance of God's rule, (Gen 2:17 & Gen 3:3) "Don't eat fruit from the tree in the center of the garden", waxed old, and over time, the lines became hazy. Adam and Eve, knowing God's instructions, willingly chose to disobey. This act of will, exposed them to unknown and unimaginable consequences. They had no idea what God's instructions were protecting them from – so they willingly disobeyed Him, and suffered terrible loss and pain.
Now, come back in time with me and remember - God offered perfect, simple "help" before it all hit the fan, by telling them "Don't eat that".
These very basic instructions were actually priceless treasure! But Adam and Eve

turned away from the treasure, and went with their worthless, counterproductive, "free will" experiment.

I said all that to make a very important point. People do this constantly. We've all done this.
That doesn't make it OK, and it never will. At the same time, it definitely muddies the water for the millions of people seeking "HELP!"
I know from personal experience, people settle for terrible results in their lives, in their walk with God, in their families, and in their careers – But never again, do I want to suffer unimaginable consequences. So, I willingly choose to fight and keep the treasure of God's truth front and center in my life, shining bright for all to see. And to the best of my ability, I keep my ridiculous "free will" chained to the wall so it doesn't hurt me or anyone else.

Psalms 121:2 NKJV
"My help comes from the Lord, Who made Heaven and Earth."

My Prayer:
Oh, God help me!
Lord, please forgive me for not treasuring Your instructions at times, and help me never to disregard the subtle way You offer me the help I need before I even need it. Help me to see the value in Your instructions, and help me to bridle my flesh and my mind so I don't injure and hinder my own progress.
Thank You God for loving me, and saving me.

In the name of The Lord Jesus Christ, Amen

DAY 2

THE CODE?

In the famous pirate movies, it's portrayed as if pirates live by some mysterious pirate's code. But when circumstances make sticking to the code less profitable, or inconvenient, well, now - the code is only a suggestion...

I need to warn you, inconvenience is never an acceptable reason for rejecting God's help.
God is ALWAYS available to help through His Spirit, His Word, and His people - but mankind has perpetually, and does continually reject God's help. Why?
Because that "free will" (the freedom to choose) sees simplicity and responsibility as lame and inconvenient.

Even in my own life, the very sad, very true reality is - I had to burn up every resource that I had before I turned to God. I lived with the pedal to the metal, and by the early age of nineteen, I had burned up all my fuel. I was done.

I didn't know it at the time, but our family was so broken, that multiple (6) tragedies and overdoses were going to occur in my family within the next decade. I wasn't the only one needing help. Decades later, I am so thankful I didn't self-destruct. Back then, life was treacherous, and I didn't know God, or go to church. Life just seemed to be hopeless, pointless, and painful.

I've heard psychiatrists and phycologists suggest that our gene pool was bent toward self-destruction. But having lived through it personally, I can tell you first hand, by experience, it's not genetic - it's demonic.

This verse from the Bible helped me so much...

Ephesians 6:12 NKJV
"We do not wrestle against flesh and blood, but against principalities, against powers, against the rulers of the darkness of this age, against spiritual hosts of wickedness in the heavenly places."
WHAT?
Do you remember the terrible phrase, "The devil made me do it?"

The truth is...
I was getting lots of *help* destroying myself. I guarantee it wasn't the Holy Spirit telling me to drop out of school, get wasted every day, and flush my life down the toilet.
This scripture truly enlightened me because I knew, down deep inside, that I wasn't *that* stupid. I was getting lots of "help".
Did you know that Jesus warns us about this?

John 10:10 NKJV
The thief (Satan) does not come except to steal, and to kill, and to destroy. I have come that they may have life, and that they may have it more abundantly.

There are evil plots at hand, not only to drag us away from God, but also to keep us from seeing His love and instructions as helpful.
Did you know, if someone offers you help and you can't see it as help, (regardless of how excellent the help is) you just might reject it? Unfortunately, that is rampant in today's society.

I BELIEVE MY HELP COMES FROM THE LORD
David wrote this thousands of years ago, just for you and me.

Psalms 121:2 NKJV
"My help comes from the Lord, Who made Heaven and Earth."

My prayer:
Oh God, help me!
Lord, help me to turn my back on the enemy's plan of destruction and fully embrace the help you have for me. Forgive me if I have rejected your loving kindness in the past, and help me to set aside anything and everything that would hinder me from receiving the help you have for me today, and in the future. Help me to see and accept the wonderful help you are providing. Help me to embrace your priceless instructions. Thank you for your patience and loving kindness! Thank you for helping me!

In the name of The Lord Jesus Christ, Amen

Day 3

LEARNING
(We ALL have to learn)

I had to learn that "MY IDEA OF HELP" wasn't always accurate. Don't miss this...

I learned, I have to allow my perceptions to be adjusted by God and His Word. I had to humble myself or be destroyed, not by God, but by self. Although difficult, I had to admit to God that my ideas and expectations were wrong.

How did I know my ideas and expectations were wrong? Because the results I was getting were repetitively, undeniably hideous.

I had to take many steps back, (and I mean MANY) and allow God to show me how things work.

Just one tiny example:
I thought as a 7 day a week alcoholic and drug addict, I needed God to cut the chains of addiction in my life. Plain and simple, I WAS WRONG.

When I finally humbled myself and genuinely cried out to God for help, He did something completely different. God began healing the pain, hopelessness, and brokenness deep inside of me. At the same time, He began filling the emptiness I carried with me everywhere I went. Now, some of these things took years, but instantly, I didn't need or want the substances that I thought were "helping" me make it through life's daily miseries. When it came to my substance abuse, my mind and emotions were so wrong that they led me to the literal end of myself. And trying to find the easy way out was killing me.

I wrote this line in one of my songs: "*My fingers have healed, but they're scarred from the climb*".

Point being, easy was not on the menu. For some reason, our uneducated, undisciplined flesh wants to be rescued from EVERYTHING uncomfortable. Our flesh perpetually wants comfort without responsibility.
We have to let God help us the way He knows we need it, and not dictate to Him what we want.
Please! Be careful, don't try to tell God what to do. He knows what you need and you don't.

James 4:10 NKJV
"Humble yourselves in the sight of the Lord, and He will lift you up."

When we humble ourselves, it's an act of surrender. No matter how long you serve

God, your flesh (and my flesh) will have its own ideas about how things "should be". We have to put God on the throne of our hearts and bow down to Him. But beware - our free will, flesh, and carnality will often raise objections to some of the most simple, practical beneficial actions we can take...

- Praying about everything
- Going Through challenges worshipping God
- Growing strong and wise through adversity
- Committing to Church (for real) and benefiting from Bible teachings and spiritual family

Note: God will *help* you find the right church if you let Him. As a teenager and a baby Christian, I drove 40 minutes each way for a good church. Don't be a wimp, everything is at stake.

- Fighting the good fight of faith

- Spending time in Gods' Word - your two-edged sword
- Giving of your time and resources; being generous like your Father in Heaven
- Learning (memorizing) & Standing on Gods promises

As you read these did your flesh squirm, object, throw excuses, or make up some stupid lie to avoid responsibility?

It happens to the best of us.
What matters is, WHAT ARE YOU GONNA "DO" ABOUT IT?

My prayer:
Oh God, help me!
Lord, help me to yield to your ways and ideas. Help me to be more like you, and less like the flaky world. Help me not to try and make You do things my way. Help me to have the courage to do what I know I

should do, and help me learn to rein in my selfish will, resistance and excuses.
Thank you for loving me so much! Thank you for your incredible mercy and faithfulness!!!

In the name of The Lord Jesus Christ,
Amen

Day 4

LORD, I WISH NOT TO SWIMMETH
(In a thick British accent)

The drowning Christian cries out to God.
God throws said Christian a life ring to save him from certain destruction.
Mr Christian doesn't "feel" like swimming six feet to save his own life. THAT'S THE FLESH, and our flesh is ridiculous.

After serving God a few years, I just decided to look at my flesh and carnality as a bad child (that may never grow up or move out) in need of constant discipline. So, until Heaven, I will have to correct, wrangle, and *with deadly force* apprehend this unpleasant part of who I am, and require of it, it's most acceptable compliance; not just for me, but for everyone around me as well.

God puts help exactly where we need it. But, the more fleshy and ungodly we are - the more it looks like "God's not trying to help at all!"

God is true, loving, gracious, and faithful. But He will never give in to *my* flesh.
If any human being thinks that God should cater to their flesh, they will NEVER get the help they need, even though it is always 100%, available.

Beware, once the whining, complaining flesh realizes it can't manipulate God - it sets up house on misery mountain, coveting what everyone else has, as if life's not fair, God's not fair, and "nobody knows the trouble I've seen".
That's the flesh.

Christian-
If you don't really believe your help comes from the Lord, you will somehow live as if ALL help is created equal. Meaning, "help

options" from anywhere are to be considered. Our fleshy free will devalues the help God has for us, and, in turn, calls all help equal in its origin. *WHY?*
Because help from God is simple and always requires responsibility.
Our flesh is seeking Fancy & Easy, or let's face it...
Academically, medically, and theologically Complicated & never remedied – the flesh clings to defects accepted as a disorders, disease, permanent emotional fracture, or genetic condition that doesn't go away, just have to live with it (and take my meds). If society says its not fixable, well then.
I say this, If I'm going to endure any "condition" with no remedy, let it be the cross God has for me to bear for His Kingdom only. Otherwise, I want all the help I can possibly get from God Himself. I want to be willing to exchange suffering for growth and forward motion.
Our flesh is lazy, selfish, and controlling.

It considers itself brilliant. The sooner you learn this, and stand up to the brat inside of you – Help is on the way!!!

Proverbs 26:15-16 NKJV
"The lazy man buries his hand in the bowl; It wearies him to bring it back to his mouth. The lazy man is wiser in his own eyes Than seven men who can answer sensibly."

My prayer:

Oh God, help me!

Lord, help me to rise up and put my flesh aside. When it comes to spiritual things, help me not to be lazy. Help me to trust you and accept responsibility for my actions and results, especially when my flesh makes a mess of things.

Thank You God for always being there for me. Thank You God for never giving up on me. Thank you for strength and wisdom.

In the name of The Lord Jesus Christ, Amen

Day 5

DO YOU REALLY BELIEVE YOUR HELP COMES FROM THE LORD? (This is huge)

Because if you don't *believe* your help comes from the Lord, you will try anything.

Hmmm, I need some help!
Well, stop and think about this question for me:

In your life, is God's help on the same shelf as all your other "options"?

Before you give yourself four and a half stars -
Do you run to God or people?
Do you complain or pray?
Do you worship or wine? Or Whine?
I'm throwing out some framework because people won't think deeply enough about that question unless prodded.

Hopefully that's not the case...
Because God is continually trying to help you, perpetually trying to build you!

When we don't set God's help apart – we live undervaluing the "spiritual" and over valuing the "natural". At the same time, you must see yourself as important to God or you can easily undervalue yourself. When we don't see ourselves in the proper light, we can be our own worst enemy.

Psalms 139:17-18 NKJV
"How precious also are Your thoughts to me, O God! How great is the sum of them! If I should count them, they would be more in number than the sand; When I awake, I am still with You."

You must know that you matter to God and shouldn't just gather help from anywhere. People continually get the wrong help from the wrong sources and that's very sad.

Think about this:
IF you were a car.
You would ALWAYS have to have very specific parts to keep you in good running condition.
Not just any parts can be grabbed and bolted on. It doesn't work that way.
Our help comes from the Lord, maker of Heaven and Earth. Yep - He's our "manufacturer" and our parts are "specific".

Be honest, can you look at your life and see that you run to God?
Do you cling to Him?
Is your confidence in Him?

2 Kings 18:5 AMP
"Hezekiah trusted in and relied confidently on the Lord, the God of Israel."

Do you turn to God in all things?

People often respond: "Of course not, I don't have to turn to God for "everything". Who does that?"

There are people in the Bible from beginning to end that did. And they got different results from everyone else. Consider Joshua and Caleb, and their "million to two" odds. I'll take that bet. Just remember, when we turn to God and cling to Him, we shouldn't get hideous results over, and over, and over, and over.

There are people all over the world, who are getting incredible results from their faith in Christ. Some of them face the harshest of circumstances, genuinely impoverished - living in countries that it's illegal to claim Christianity - beaten and imprisoned for believing in Christ, and they cling to Him with all their hearts: with joy, and peace, and stoutheartedness; they are unshakable.

Their faith and hope cannot be stripped from them. BUT, there's also what I call,

Lionel Ritchie Christians. They're only in, if it's "Easy Like Sunday Morning".

My Prayer:
Oh God, help me!
Lord, help me not to be lazy with spiritual things. Help me not to fake like I depend on you. Help me to be the real deal inside and out.
Thank you for always listening to me.
Thank you for helping me grow forward.
Thank you for forgiveness.
Thank you for peace.

In the name of The Lord JESUS Christ,
Amen

Day 6

SOME HELP ISN'T HELP AT ALL

When I was very young, I played biddy football. We were tiny. Our uniforms didn't fit. Our helmets wobbled on our little heads. And we bounced off of each other, barely even understanding the plays. I was seven.
Coach Sid Stone taught me...
"When the going gets tough, the tough get going!"
At the time, I thought that meant, "run, even if you're tired", cause coach always said it when we were running. Regardless of my lack of life experience at the age of seven, it helped.

All grown up, and serving God...
"When the going gets tough, the tough get going TO GOD". Now I'm a pastor.
How'd you do that?

I have, and shall continue to, run to God, over, and over, and over, and over. I know I don't have a chance without God.
How'd you get off of drugs and alcohol?
I ran to God.
What about your family, aren't they a mess?
Yep, only God, ONLY GOD!

MY HELP COMES FROM THE LORD!

I can't live the life I live without continual help from Him. Not only how God rescued me from where I was, not only to get me where I am, but also to keep me going forward. Remember, God's help is simple and requires responsibility.

Everyone wants to help, right?
If I accepted the help that some friends and family offered me when I became a Christian (it may have been from the kindness of their hearts) it sure wouldn't have helped me. It would have ruined me,

made things more difficult, and polluted my process. Please be very careful. We all love our friends and family, but they're not God - I'm just telling you. One of my parents attacked and wrongly criticized the church I went to. One of my brothers didn't want me to quit smoking weed with him. He said he hated the fact that I was reading my Bible and going to church. Some lifelong friends told me I could go to church and still party my brains out with them. My high school principal told me, "Trust me Mr Gray, Jesus didn't help you, you just came to your senses".

They were all trying to "help". But if I listened to any of them, it would have shipwrecked me.
Sweet wonderful people will always offer unsolicited advice - I don't tell them they're Wackadoodle (sometimes I do).

But most of the time, I just say "thank you very much" and let it go in one ear, and out the other.
Know this, I spent years in counseling getting excellent help, but there's a lot of help out there that isn't excellent. Please be careful.

My help comes from the Lord, and so does yours.
Put God first, and be careful how much help you allow from people who don't know God or His plan for your life. They may mean well, but that doesn't mean you should listen to them.

Psalms 119:2 NKJV
"Blessed are those who keep His testimonies, Who seek Him with the whole heart!"

My prayer:
Oh God, help me!
Lord there are so many voices and ideas available. As I seek you, please help me to find YOU and not everything else. Help me to sort through all the options and keep you first in everything.
Help me to know when I'm being offered tainted advice. Thank you for helping me, watching over me, and protecting me! Thank you for being there for me. Thank you for helping me over, and over.

In the name of The Lord Jesus Christ,
Amen

Day 7

BELIEVE & KNOW

John 6:63-69
"The Spirit alone gives eternal life. Human effort accomplishes nothing. And the very words I have spoken to you are spirit and life. But some of you do not believe Me." (For Jesus knew from the beginning which ones didn't believe, and he knew who would betray him.) Then He said,
"That is why I said that people can't come to Me unless the Father gives them to Me. At this point many of His disciples turned away and deserted Him. Then Jesus turned to the Twelve and asked, "Are you also going to leave?" Simon Peter replied,
"Lord, to whom would we go? You have the words that give eternal life.
WE BELIEVE, AND WE KNOW You are the Holy One of God."

The "Walk Away" attitude has plagued humanity: I can't overcome my difficulty so I give up on God.

Many of His disciples deserted Him. The word *disciples* there, scares me. It scares me because it wasn't the masses, it wasn't the throng - on this day, many of His disciples deserted Him.

Just because something is complicated and difficult, doesn't mean it's OK to quit.

If I don't understand something, if it's harder than I ever expected - I am not allowed to quit.

I LOVE how Peter responded to Jesus. He said, "TO WHOM WOULD WE GO?"

This is sober perfection, and you better be ready to answer this question on any given day of your life as you walk with God.
Turning back is not an option,
#1 Because I *believe* it's not an option.
#2 Because Jesus has the Words of Life.
To whom would we go, right?

The next thing Peters says seals the deal...
**WE BELIEVE & KNOW
YOU ARE THE HOLY ONE OF GOD!**

You gotta love it! Whether the truth hurts or not, it always helps! There's no better help on the planet, in the universe, in all the galaxies!!!
You found your Creator and Savior - STAY THE COURSE to the end. Rejoice! Your searching is over, but on this journey, you will be tested.
Don't worry or be afraid... God will help you.

My prayer:
Oh God, help me!
Lord, help me never to turn my back on You.
Help me never to walk away from You, Church, or Your Word! Help me to stand in any storm. Help me to press through hard seasons even when I don't understand,

even when it seems impossible! Help me Lord, when things get complicated.
Thank You for embracing me. Thank You for helping me figure things out one day at a time. Thank You for being here with me right this second. Praise You for every good thing in my life!

In the name of The Lord Jesus Christ, Amen

Day 8

GOD DOESN'T GIVE UP ON US

Some of our perceptions (the things we "think") about God and our difficulties are wrong.
We all have a BUNCH of learning to do, and it's during challenges, and through difficulties that we find the most valuable information and lessons. All the learning and growth isn't just for you.

This is heavy duty, mature Christian information: God wants us to conquer, and by His Grace (undeserved favor) we can have real victory. But just like we desperately needed Christ to finish His mission on the cross, other people need us to find victory in our walk of faith. Yes, people are depending on you to stay the course.

2 Corinthians 12:7-9 NLT (Paul speaking)
"Even though I have received such wonderful revelations from God. So, to keep me from becoming proud, I was given a thorn in my flesh, a messenger from Satan to torment me and keep me from becoming proud. Three different times I begged the Lord to take it away. Each time He said, "My grace is (sufficient) all you need. My power works best in weakness." So now I am glad to boast about my weaknesses, so that the power of Christ can work through me."

Wow - this is very sobering.
Our responsibility to God, ourselves, and everyone around us, is vast. Trusting in God is never just about me. There are people that are depending on you to stay the course - just like we were depending on Paul to fight the good fight of faith.
I don't think Paul knew how important this would be 2,000 years later. So, I don't expect we genuinely understand right now

how important it is to NEVER give up! Stay the course! Finish the mission!
    God won't give up on you,
    so don't you ever give up on you!

My Prayer:
Oh God, help me!
Lord, please help me to know the difference between self-induced struggles and struggles that you assign. I know that no assignment from you is wasted. Help me to remember that people I haven't even met yet are counting on me to do my part. Help me to take responsibility and grow through adversity. Help me to be humble, and clear minded when things get difficult.
Thank You for Your presence in my life. Thank You for saving me and holding my hand. Thank You for Your never-ending Love!

    In the name of The Lord Jesus Christ, Amen

Day 9

NEGLIGENCE CAUSES PAIN

Rom 8:31
If God is for us, who can be against us?

I love this passage, but I require myself to answer the question that is being posed.

And I rephrase it with parentheses to amplify the truth that I've come to know over the decades.

If God is for me (and He is), who can be against me (and win)? And I answer: Everyone and everything, including my own flesh - can be against me - But NOTHING can defeat me with God, Nothing.

Now, I said all that to say this...
One of the greatest challenges I have faced as a Christian - is me. My flesh always

wants its way, and *always* seems to put in its two cents.
My flesh doesn't like sacrifice.
My flesh is selfish, not selfless.
So, while I happily jump on God's bandwagon, my flesh still causes complications that can bring on very unpleasant lessons. I must learn to depend on God to get me where I'm going, and I must learn to correct my flesh when it wants to neglect important spiritual things.

My prayer:
Oh God, help me!
Lord, help me never to allow my flesh to trick me into neglect. Help me never to neglect the things You want me to embrace and take care of.
Help me never to neglect Your Word. Help me to avoid the pain that comes from neglect by refusing to disregard important little things that matter a lot. Thank You for always helping me! Thank You for Your patience and faithfulness - they are

priceless to me. Thank You for helping me become aware of things I have neglected, and forgive me for not seeing it until now. Lord, I love You and need You in my life every day.

In the name of The Lord Jesus Christ, Amen

Day 10

SHAMELESS PERSISTENCE

Luke 11:5-10 NLT
"Then, teaching them
more about prayer, Jesus used this story:
"Suppose you went to a friend's house at
midnight, wanting to borrow three loaves
of bread. You say to him, A friend of mine
has just arrived for a visit and I have
nothing for him to eat.' And suppose he
calls out from his bedroom, 'Don't bother
me. The door is locked for the night, and
my family and I are all in bed. I can't help
you? But I tell you this--though he won't do
it for friendship's sake, if you keep
knocking long enough, he will get up and
give you whatever you need because of
your shameless persistence.
"And so I tell you, keep on asking, and you
will receive what you ask for. Keep on
seeking, and you will find. Keep on
knocking, and the door will be opened to

you. For everyone who asks, receives. Everyone who seeks, finds. And to everyone who knocks, the door will be opened."

This is SO important:
Everyday people try to gauge their results by measuring their efforts.
I'm warning you right now. Don't stop trying when you "feel" you've put forth enough effort.
You press until you get the results God has for you.

If you get nothing else from this entire devotional GET THIS!

You must have faith to persist. Everyone tries a little, but only a few people press, and push, and ask, and seek, and knock! You be the one that pushes past keeping track of the price, and go after God with everything you have to work with.

Your shameless persistence is what will produce the results you need. And beware of advice from people who refuse to try as hard as Jesus says we should. They are everywhere, whining and complaining and bringing other people down. Don't let their flesh drag you down and pollute your heart and mind.

YOU...
Show up
Press in
Stay faithful
Pay the price
Give your all
Stand strong
Hold on tight
Refuse to lose
YOU show Shameless Persistence!!!

My Prayer:
Oh God, help me!
Lord, help me to go the distance when many things try to stop me. Help me to find my shameless persistence! Help me to continue to reach for the victory You have for me regardless of feelings and naysayers.
Thank You for wanting the best for me.
Thank You for sending Jesus to show us what shameless persistence really is!
Thank You for caring about my life and strengthening me!
Thank You for helping me.

In the name of The Lord Jesus Christ,
Amen

Day 11

WHERE DO I START? "I DON'T KNOW"

Luke 11:9 NLT
(Jesus said)
Keep on asking
Keep on seeking
Keep on knocking

I want to share one of my secret weapons for success with you. It's so simple that it's overlooked every day by many people.

There have been many times over the years that I genuinely didn't know what was next, or what to say, or what to do, or what to pray.
Honestly telling God that you don't know is the perfect place to begin getting excellent help.
Jesus said, "Keep on asking", and His instructions should not be ignored.

1 Peter 5:5
God gives grace to the humble.

When I'm struggling with ANYTHING that is stopping me, confusing me, or baffling me - I step back in how I'm approaching God and the circumstance. There are days that I find myself in new territory and I truly don't know what to ask, or how to approach or look at a situation.

I tell God, "I don't even know what to ask" and I ask God to help me ask the right questions.
I ask God to help me pray the way I need to pray.
I ask God to help me think the way He needs me to think in order to move forward His way.

Here's what I mean, this has become a repetitive exercise: I tell God, "Lord, I've never been here before". I remind God and I remind myself, at this adventurous moment in my life, I have never been this age, married this long, with kids this age, with choices like these - with this many years behind, and God only knows how many years ahead. I tell God that I don't know what tomorrow holds, but I know He does. I ask Him to help me ask for help because I simply don't know if there's things I'm not seeing. I don't know if there's things I'm not doing or things I need to start doing, so I ask for help. I've found that asking God to help me *ask for help,* has turned many of my frustrations into fresh new experiences and successes that only God could give me.

As I look back, all I can say is "Thank You Lord!", because I'm so glad I asked. I'm not shy about not understanding everything. I just do exactly like Jesus said. I ask and keep asking.

My prayer:
Oh God, help me!
Lord, help me to know when I am on the wrong page, or out of step with You. Help me to ask the right questions about my needs so I don't get stuck off path. I know I need Your help to change and to grow. Help me to see where to make the adjustments I need to make. Thank You Lord for making the help I need available. Thank you for leading me beside still waters and refreshing me with Your involvement and providence.
Thank You that Your help is always a prayer away!

In the name of The Lord Jesus Christ,
Amen

Day 12

LIVE BY FAITH, DON'T DRAW BACK

Hebrews 10:38-39 KJV
"Now the just shall live by faith; But if anyone draws back, My soul has no pleasure in him. But we are not of those who draw back to perdition, but of those who believe to the saving of the soul."

Perdition means destruction - basically, we don't retreat to our own demise. God can't take pleasure in me if I draw back, back pedal, give up, or throw in the towel.

Now I've seen people act like "that's God's problem", because they just can't go on; they just can't take it anymore! (people's drama can be very real and uncontrollable in their own minds)
Every day, people do the wrong thing over and over, then expect God to give them

victory and success. Sadly, they were ignorantly doomed from the start.

If we refuse God's help, or refuse to ask for help, or refuse to do it God's way - God will definitely allow us to suffer. We see this with an entire generation of The Children of Israel being left in the desert to die. They refused to believe God, so God refused them from entering the promised land. He did many miracles and set them free from slavery, but from there, it was up to them to trust God, and go after what He had for them.

It's sad, and I believe the Israelites constantly polluted each other with fear, distrust, doubt, and disbelief. The beautiful thing is that the ones who believed, got help, even if it was only two of them. With His help, I don't have to fail over and over and give up. Trusting in God, there's always some "God Resource" that can impact my situation, and get me winning again. Remember, His mercies are new every morning. I choose to live by faith, and in doing so, I shackle myself to God. He is my hope and unlimited help in times of trouble.

My prayer:
Oh God, help me!
Lord, help me to accept Your help and Your call to blessed trust and obedience. Help me to always agree with You. If You say I can, I can! Help me not to be destabilized by fear and feelings. Help me never to listen to people who refuse to trust You. Thank You God for promising me victory. Thank You for helping me move into the blessed existence You have for me - no matter how many giants I have to slay. Thank You for thinking higher of me than I think of myself.
I love You and need You.

In the name of The Lord Jesus Christ,
Amen

Day 13

A HELPER

John 14:15-16 NKJV (Jesus speaking)
"If you love Me, keep My commandments. And I will pray the Father, and He will give you another Helper, that He may abide with you forever".

God's Holy Spirit is our "Forever Helper".
All my help comes from the Lord.
He loves me and wants me to succeed.

I may not have all the answers, but...
MY HELP COMES FROM THE LORD

Our government has issues, but...
MY HELP COMES FROM THE LORD

The landscape of society is changing rapidly, but...
MY HELP COMES FROM THE LORD

I heard something disturbing, but…
MY HELP COMES FROM THE LORD

There's trouble brewing, but…
MY HELP COMES FROM THE LORD

I need answers I don't have, but…
MY HELP COMES FROM THE LORD

The doctor gave me a negative report, but…
MY HELP COMES FROM THE LORD

I struggle all the time, but…
MY HELP COMES FROM THE LORD

In all things, and at all times – God's Holy Spirit is our Forever Helper! God knew, we would need all the help we can get, so He arranged to give us the best helper that ever existed!

Matt 28:20 NKJV (Jesus speaking)
Lo, I am with you always, even to the end of the age. Amen

My help comes from the Lord NO MATTER WHAT! He's with me NO MATTER WHERE, and when does He help me? ALWAYS

My prayer:
Oh God, help me!
Lord, thank You sending another helper into our lives. Help me to accept Your help on your terms. Help me never to cling to my own plans if they conflict with Your plans. Help me to turn to You with everything. Help me to surrender my life to Your brilliant plans for the future, and never cling to the ashes of my past. Thank You for sending Your precious Holy Spirit to help me! Thank You for always being with me - to the end of the age.

In the name of The Lord Jesus Christ, Amen

Day 14

HELP WANTED!

When companies need help, they put a sign in the window. They communicate that they have a need, and welcome people to receive financial benefits in exchange for fulfilling business appropriate tasks and duties. This has been normal for a very long time.

Something that bewilders me, is, Christians wanting help and not giving the job to God. They're supposed to be living for God, and they look everywhere under Heaven (other than God) for help. All the while, their Creator, Savior, their Father in Heaven, Ever-present, King of kings - is there for them with the help they need.
Still, people consciously look past God for the world's flavor of the day in self-help, and church fads. They trust grandma more

than Jesus, and experiment with "sure to fail" options, instead of running to God. God is truly available to us all. But, don't get me wrong, God is not a butler or a servant. He is the King of Heavens Armies. Respect, reverence, and humility are a must. We have the privilege of seeking God for help. We also have the responsibility to reject all the slop that the world feeds on every day, and humble ourselves.
I must choose to clear my life of distractions, let God in, and sit with Him.

Revelation 3:20 NKJV
"Behold, I stand at the door and knock. If anyone hears My voice and opens the door, I will come in to him and dine with him, and he with Me."

We must let Jesus in.
We must cultivate intimacy with God.
If we don't treasure spending time in His presence, anything can distract us and compete with Gods place in our lives.

Nowadays, people spend time like they're "time billionaires" and won't ever run out. The worthless little distractions that don't matter at all, are wasting the priceless, irreplaceable moments that could be spent learning, growing, and building with God.

Hire God! Give Him the executive position in your life. His help is what you need.

My prayer:
Oh God, help me!
Lord, please help me to stop looking up and down, and all around, for help that I can only get from You! No one knows me like You do and no one loves me like You do - so help me to keep You first in the help department.
Help me to turn my back on harmful, corrupt help, and help me to only accept help that is true.
Thank You God for Your help! Thank You for knocking on the door of my heart, and

patiently waiting for me to come to my senses and open the door!
Thank You for wanting a relationship with me.
Thank You for pursuing me and helping me.

In the name of The Lord Jesus Christ,
Amen

Day 15

GOD'S RESUME

Did you hire God to be your helper? Maybe you're not sure God will fit into your life and help the way you want Him to.

Maybe He's over qualified.
But please, consider Him for the job.

Imagine Psalms 121 as God's Resume; look it up and read the whole chapter. It's only eight verses:

*He made Heaven and Earth
*He will not allow you to be moved
*He keeps you
*He will not slumber of sleep
*He is your keeper
*The Lord overshadows you
*He shall protect you day and night
*He will preserve you from all evil

*He shall preserve your soul
*The Lord shall preserve your going out and your coming in forevermore
Psalms 121 tells me that God should definitely get the job every single time I need help!
There aren't any candidates that are as fit for the job as God Himself, not one.

Call Him, He can work remotely and you won't regret hiring Him. He also moonlights, so He can help all your friends, family, neighbors, co-workers, and strangers you meet.

My prayer:
Oh God, help me!
Lord, help me not to turn to unqualified help!
Help me to see through the world's deceptive and false help. Help me to remember that no one is more qualified to help me than You.

Forgive me for looking to the wrong sources in the past. Thank You for many second chances.
Thank You for not disqualifying me for mistakes.
Thank You for love that overshadows my life with goodness and perfect help!

In the name of The Lord Jesus Christ, Amen

Day 16

HOW LONG DOES IT TAKE?

Sometimes it bothers me, how many times I need to hear something, read something, or see something to remember and apply it. Over the decades, I've heard many versions of the 21 days to form a good habit ideology. But for some reason that never worked for me.
I'm thankful that it works for some people. But I could go 48 days and my flesh is just waiting for day 49 to stop trying. Does anyone understand?

Proverbs 24:16 NKJV
"A righteous man may fall seven times and rise again, But the wicked shall fall by calamity."
        I fall down, I get up.
Not because I'm indestructible (I'm actually the opposite), but because my help comes from the Lord! He sent me the Holy Spirit

as the Helper.   He knocked, and I let Him in; He is my keeper, my glory and the lifter of my head.

I rise, ONLY because He helps me rise.

My prayer:
Oh God, help me!
Lord there isn't a day that goes by that I don't need something from You.
Help me to be as gracious as You are, helping others when they slip and fall.
Help me to freely give what I have freely received. Thank You for never letting me stay down. Thank You for mercy and grace to rise from struggles and stand. Thank You for letting me share your amazing devotion to us with others who need just as much help as I do. And help me to sing with joy - because I know my help comes from the Lord!

In the name of The Lord Jesus Christ,
Amen

Day 17

AN EVERYDAY CHOICE

Psalms 18:1-3 NKJV
"I will love You, O Lord, my strength. The Lord is my rock and my fortress and my deliverer; My God, my strength, in whom I will trust; My shield and the horn of my salvation, my stronghold. I will call upon the Lord, who is worthy to be praised; So shall I be saved from my enemies."

I understand it takes a close relationship with God to go to Him with everything, but how close?

I would imagine that Adam and Eve were pretty close to God. Right?
But not once did they go to God for help while being tempted.
It's my opinion (only my opinion) that Eve wasn't deceived instantly, but that, over time, and being manipulated, she ate the

forbidden fruit and shared it with Adam. Think about this one: Who counseled Cain before he murdered Abel? Well God did that's who. Perfect advice and close proximity to God doesn't necessarily mean that you're assured victory. It's more about having a humble heart.

Our flesh can be bratty. Think about how some children *REFUSE* to let you to help them because they want to do it themselves (even when they can't). They are on a mission to become "independent ". Asking God for help is an act of humility...

1 Peter 5:6 NLT
"Humble yourselves under the mighty power of God, and at the right time he will lift you up in honor."

My prayer:
Oh God, help me!
Lord, help me to cherish the privilege of depending on You.
Help me to ask You for help first and not last.
Help me not to forget that Your ways are higher than mine.
Lord, thank You so much for helping me to grow in my trust with You. I truly want to trust You with everything.
Thank You for being there every day in my life.
Lord, forgive me for jumping into things too quickly without praying or seeking Your help first. I know I need all the help I can get.
Thank You for protecting me from enemies I can't even see.

In the name of The Lord Jesus Christ,
Amen

Day 18

COME TO ME

Matthew 11:28-30 NLT
Then Jesus said, "Come to me, all of you who are weary and carry heavy burdens, and I will give you rest. Take my yoke upon you. Let Me teach you, because I am humble and gentle at heart, and you will find rest for your souls. For My yoke is easy to bear, and the burden I give you is light."

The best help is obviously God's prescribed help.

There are definitely times when we are simply carrying too much, doing too much, or getting overwhelmed by burdens. You can feel the compassion Jesus is offering to the whole world as He welcomes us to come to Him. What an amazing Savior!

Sadly, many people have lived and died, never having their burdens lifted.
Again, it takes a humble heart to accept such help.
I for one, would rather be humble and helped, than independent and exhausted to death. But there have been days that it took falling to my knees under a heavy load - before I even realized, it was too much. But Jesus lets us try, He lets us put forth our best effort, He lets us strive - He wants us in the game. But He's also right there to help when we come to the end of ourselves.

With deep loving compassion, He says,
"Come to me"

My prayer:
Oh God, help me!
Lord thank You for helping me when life, and its burdens overwhelm me. Thank You for being right there when I realize it's too

much, and thank You for lifting the load that (at some point) I shouldn't have tried to carry on my own.
Help me to welcome Your help into every area of my life. Help me in family relationships, help me in my career - never let me go. I need You always.

In the name of The Lord Jesus Christ, Amen

Day 19

THERE'S HELP & THERE'S NOT HELP

Psalms 121:1
MY HELP COMES FROM THE LORD!

When it comes to help, there are so many sources other than God and His Word. Every day people search and spend and dig to find help that isn't really help at all. I've learned...
        "There's Help!"
        And
        "There's Not Help!"
I'm not trying to be silly. I have read many books that promise help. Only to finish my reading with...
        "Not Help"
I'm not kidding. Of course, there are good, helpful books, but I have read hundreds of books, and not all books deliver.

And people try to help - not realizing, the so called help they are offering is TERRIBLE!
Some friend's suggestions for "help" have shocked me once explored.

When I really gave my life to God, accepted Jesus in my heart and was forgiven and born again - I received help from God like I'd never experienced before. And wouldn't you know it?
I had friends and family try to drag me away from God, and church, and the Bible.

When I look back at them trying to "help" me, it's terrifying. They really thought they were offering me help. All it was is help to mess up again, help to fail, help to lose my grip on God, help to stay empty, broken, and self-destructive.

It still blows my mind when I think about it. And I always thank God that I didn't listen to them.

Compounded suffering was waiting for me if I had rejected God's help and taken their help instead.

> Be careful...
> "There's Help" &
> "There's Not Help"

My prayer:
Oh God, help me!
Lord thank You for helping me see the difference between good help and bad help!
Thank You for rescuing me from the enemy's plans for destruction.
Thank You for forgiveness and healing, and for helping me like no other.
You are my fortress, my Helper, my shield!
I don't want to live without Your help.
I don't want to step into tomorrow without Your supernatural beautiful help!

Lord, at the same time, help me to offer good help to the people in my life - by guiding them to You.
Help me to help others find You;
My perfect Helper.

In the name of The Lord Jesus Christ,
Amen

Day 20

BEGGING GOD FOR HELP

I asked Jesus into my heart at a friend's house - sitting at the dining room table. God definitely helped me, saved me, and began healing my broken heart. I received a genuine miracle. But now, I had to go to church.

Personally, I had a hard heart and a very critical attitude when it came to church. I truly thought all preachers were crazy, and before becoming a Christian, I mocked preachers and Christians.
Not gonna lie, the thought of going to church was a very scary subject for me. I began BEGGING God to help me, and I mean BEGGING!!!

>   I was terrified
> I was full of distrust

> I felt vulnerable
> I could think of a thousand
> reasons not to go to church

First, my friend invited me to her church, this seemed harmless, so I went with her. The church service was a bit rowdy and super emotional. With God's help, I instantly knew this wasn't the church for me. No questions asked - I knew it. Deep inside I knew.

The problem? My church fears were vigorously reinforced and I was very disappointed.

I kindly told my friend thank you, and moved on. All the while, BEGGING God to help me find a church. This was a difficult process. Obeying God can be extremely challenging to our senses - our feelings can be SO strong.

I AM BEGGING GOD FOR HELP THOUGH

I prayerfully started looking for the church God wanted me to attend.
Note: Don't let some chicken-hearted, damaged person tell you that you don't have to go to church to know God. I met God through a friend - I trusted God to lead me to the right spiritual family and I learned the Bible and grew at church. Let God help you & go to church.

Acts 2:46-47 NKJV
"So, continuing daily with one accord in the temple, and breaking bread from house to house, they ate their food with gladness and simplicity of heart, praising God and having favor with all the people. And the Lord added to the church daily those who were being saved."

Wow, they went to temple every day back in Bible times. I visited three different churches while BEGGING God to help me - and He did!

Proverbs 3:5-6
Trust in the Lord with all your heart and lean not on your own understanding.
In all your ways acknowledge Him, and He will direct your path.

My prayer:
Oh God, help me!
Lord, help me never to put my feelings and society's opinions above or before You.
Help me to trust You. I know that You are trustworthy, but there are things I genuinely fear. Help me God! I'm BEGGING You! Help Me Please!
Lord, forgive my excuses and resistance, and help me to let You lead me on the proper path.
Thank You for putting up with me!
Thank You for loving me - in spite of me!
Thank You for having a special path for me that leads to stability and blessing!

In the name of The Lord Jesus Christ, Amen

Day 21

DON'T GIVE UP, ASK GOD FOR HELP!

When it came to the subject of church, I was very bitter.

As a brand-new baby Christian who knew nothing... I kept telling God, "Preachers are all crazy". Well, that's what I thought.
And I felt like I had to tell God this over and over while BEGGING Him to help me find a church.
I was begging because I knew that I had to move forward, but I was going to have to trust God and "some" people.
You see, I grew up in a household with conflicting denominations. My mom and her family were catholic. My dad was country club.
But when I was six, my dad became a believer and began attending a different church than my mom.

Some really good things came from dad becoming a Christian. He stopped being an alcoholic, he stopped gambling, and he stopped chasing women. Sadly, He remained violent and frustrated at home. His "family" toolbox was completely empty. He didn't know how to be a husband, or a dad. This is understandable, his mom was married five times, so dysfunction (as they say in golf) is par for the course.

He didn't stop fighting with my mom, and he didn't stop ditching work for golf. But he definitely had "some" real God miracles in his life. Unfortunately, church became a war in our household. Dad had an extreme personality. He went to many churches and had memberships at all of them. I never understood it, and our family suffered terribly. No doubt, God saved my dad, but he never got help. Our family just stayed a mess.

All that said, maybe you can see how I connected some of our family's issues with church, and preachers. Honestly, I wanted NOTHING to do with God or church or preachers. I was bitter, and all that mess confused the daylights out of me as a kid. I hated my dad for his rage at home, and my hate compounded with his wild spirituality. Well, now I was grown, and it was time to let all that go and do things right. One thing's for sure, I knew how "not to do it".

Acts 3:19 NKJV
Repent therefore and be converted, that your sins may be blotted out, so that times of refreshing may come from the presence of the Lord."

I needed the refreshing God had for me. I had to ask God to forgive me for the life altering hate I was carrying. I had to forgive my dad regardless of his mistakes. To this day, this is was the hardest thing I ever had to do...
        BUT GOD HELPED ME

I forgave my dad, and knew I had to find a good church with trustworthy leadership. I had already seen how having the wrong spiritual leaders in your life can really mess you up.
I needed a Bible believing, God loving, genuine Christian church - and God helped me find one.

I needed a good church if I was going to have a good life. Church is where I met a handful of amazing people that became lifelong friends.
I met my wife and after decades of marriage we've only had 4 fights. To me, that's a miracle. I know God has helped both of us enormously!
Matthew 6:14-15 NKJV
"For if you forgive men their trespasses, your heavenly Father will also forgive you. But if you do not forgive men their trespasses, neither will your Father forgive your trespasses."

(I know this is hard. Ask for Help)
My prayer:
Oh God, help me!
Lord, You and I both know I need help. Please God, help me to rise above the hurt, distrust, and fear. Help me to forgive everyone who has ever done me wrong. Help me to let go of the burdens I have held on to. I release them in Jesus' name. Help me to know when I need to revisit forgiveness, releasing people that have hurt me. Help me to lay aside all bitterness. Thank You for forgiving me. Thank You for healing my broken heart and helping me to learn from ALL the mistakes that have impacted my life negatively.
Thank You for holding me together.
I love and need You!

In the name of The Lord Jesus Christ,
Amen

Day 22

WILL GOD HELP YOU?

Read this a few times slowly because it is definitely treasure:

Isaiah 41:10 NKJV
"Fear not, for I am with you; Be not dismayed, for I am your God. I will strengthen you, **yes, I will help you**. I will uphold you with My righteous right hand."

Did you know that many people don't believe God will help them?

But you just read it for yourself...
"YES, GOD WILL HELP YOU"

Please be careful. Don't let people tell you different from God.
People all over the world are making this mistake daily. Don't be a casualty.

Don't go along with ANY ideology that devalues God's Word in your life.
It's true and sad, some people go through decades of misery before they finally, humble themselves and ask God for help.

Do we have to come to a place of total desperation before we ask God for help?
No - but our carnal mind can be so stubborn, it will hold out until we come to the complete end of ourselves.
As a Christian, I choose to live at the end of myself, ready to turn to God at any instant. Why suffer more than I need to?
I haven't arrived yet. Even though I spent years suffering, I still take the scenic route sometimes. One thing's for sure, I get there a lot quicker than I used to. Please don't ever wonder, "Will God help me?"
YES, HE WILL HELP YOU!

We all have friends, family, coworkers, neighbors, and strangers in our lives...
Will God help them?

WILL GOD HELP THEM?

Yes, but it's kind of like on an airplane... Put your oxygen mask on first, then help others. Right? As you receive help from God, you should help everyone around you get help from God.

My prayer:
Oh God, help me!
Lord, thank You for the simplicity of this passage. Thank You for saying point blank, "Yes, I will help you!" Please help me to put all doubt in check when I don't know how You're going to help. Thank You for watching over me, and including me in Your plan to help others. Help me to know when it's time to roll up my sleeves and get to work helping someone else.
Thank You for making it so simple.

In the name of The Lord Jesus Christ,
Amen

Day 23

SERVE GOD? OR SELF SERVE?

This is Samuel speaking to the Children of Israel. They told Samuel, they want to do what's right; they want to serve God. Samuel tells them...

1 Samuel 12:21 NLT
"Don't go back to worshiping worthless idols that cannot help or rescue you--they are totally useless!"

Samuel told them,
"Stop turning to things that cannot help or rescue you!"
For some reason, people go from hot to cold in one day. Isn't it "human" to, one minute say, "Yay, I'm gonna trust God and live for Him!" But the next minute be lost in the woods spiritually?

The Children of Israel continually did this. One minute serving God, the next, worshiping Baal. This was a pagan god, an idol. Baal never did a miracle, never answered a prayer, never helped anyone, he was a statue. But Baal worship "allowed" sex outside of marriage, drunkenness, murder, and other despicable things.

Look at it this way:
Baal was like an evil step dad...
"I wanna go live with him!" WHY???
"Because he lets me do whatever I want!"

Simply put, Baal worship, was "anything goes".
Anything does not go! And God wants to help you. He doesn't want you to destroy yourself, destroy others, destroy your family, destroy your career, your finances, or your future.

God is real! He helps us, and He rescues us! The attitude "anything goes", only serves self, and cultivates certain destruction.

REMEMBER WHAT SAMUEL SAID
"Don't go back to worshiping worthless idols that cannot help or rescue you--they are totally useless!"

When you give your life to God, don't go back to living and thinking like a knucklehead!
Don't go back to clinging to the wrong people, and ideas about life. And Don't look for ways to justify poor living and pathetic behavior.
LET GOD HELP AND RESCUE YOU!

My prayer:
Oh God, help me!
Lord, help me never to go back! Help me to live in Your presence and receive Your help. Help me to grow forward and become

completely stable as a Christian. I don't want to be the one who fails or falls. Help me to trust You, and not to cling to false doctrine, or societal deception.
You are my help and my rescuer!
Thank You Lord!

In the name of The Lord Jesus Christ,
Amen

Day 24

IT TAKES FAITH

When we put other things before God, we welcome spiritual dysfunction, and instability. Sometimes we do it on purpose, eyes wide open. But other times, it can be a subtle process.
There are things that people do and say, that show that God isn't really first in their lives.
Imagine thinking God is first in your life, when He isn't - that's scary. But It's probably more common than you think. Our faith walk needs to be front and center.

Romans 1:16-17 NKJV
(Paul to the church in Rome)
"I am not ashamed of the gospel of Christ, for it is the power of God to salvation for everyone who believes, for the Jew first and also for the Greek. For in it the

righteousness of God is revealed from faith to faith; as it is written, "The just shall live by faith."

We are all coerced by the world to seek everything but God. Our flesh, the enemy, and the world call to us like pirates gold. Without even thinking, people change course, and put their trust in things other than God.
They put their HOPE in things other than God. They collect spiritual information from sources other than the Bible. When the terrible results come in, it's hard to explain that their "idea" of God's firstness is off.

I am not saying that we can't acquire help and information from multiple sources, but I am saying, If you're gonna live for God, it takes faith! And faith is a narrow path. We must have faith in God and faith in His Word. Faith is what we believe - so it's the sum of our devotion to God...

- It takes faith to put God first
- It takes faith to keep God first
- It takes faith to passionately seek God
- It takes faith to turn your back on the world and all of its "opportunities"

Romans 1:17 NKJV
THE JUST SHALL LIVE BY FAITH

Galatians 3:11 NKJV
THE JUST SHALL LIVE BY FAITH

Hebrews 10:38 NKJV
THE JUST SHALL LIVE BY FAITH

It takes faith.

My prayer:
Oh God, help me!
Lord, help me to truly believe the way You want me to believe. Help me to cultivate pure faith!

Help me to see clearly where You are in my life. And help me to make adjustments that please You. Please forgive me for being easily distracted, and help me not to make foolish excuses.

You need to be FIRST in my life, and I need Your help balancing out my life, now, and in the future.

Thank You Lord that I can ask You for help concerning anything. Thank You for touching my heart and helping me.

In the name of The Lord Jesus Christ, Amen

Day 25

I WANT GOD RESULTS

Matthew 4:4 NKJV (Jesus said)
"It is written, 'Man shall not live by bread alone, but by every word that proceeds from the mouth of God."

In order to get "God Results", His Word must be flowing through my life. Jesus is the Word made flesh. So as I fill my heart with The Word, I'm soaking my heart and mind with Jesus.

Romans 10:17 NKJV
Faith comes by hearing, and hearing by the Word of God.

Check out what David said...
Ps 119:105 NKJV
Your Word is a lamp to my feet and a light to my path.

Straight up - the world is a dark place. I must have God's Word in my heart. I must learn, believe, and stand on His promises.

Let's be practical / take inventory...
- Am I learning God's Word?
- Am I living and applying God's Word?

Jesus tells us the truth! We can't just live on food. We need Gods Word every day.

I WANT GOD RESULTS!

I want to put my trust in God! I understand that some of the things people cling to, are harmful, and counterproductive. So I will ask God to help me cling to the Word of the Lord!

My help comes from the Lord, and His Word is life to me! I don't want to live like everyone else.
I don't want lame results.

I want to live trusting in God's precious promises.

I really do want God results!

My prayer:
Oh God, help me!
Lord, I see that the opportunity to get terrible results is all around me!
Please God help me not to settle for anything but Your best for me.
Thank You for giving us Your Word. Thank You for Your precious promises. Help me to learn and remember Your Word. Help me to live and share Your Word. Thank You for giving all of us something more important than food to live on. Thank You for the incredible results that are coming my way as I embrace Your Words of life on a daily basis.

In the name of The Lord Jesus Christ,
Amen

Day 26

GOD IS NOT THE AUTHOR OF CONFUSION, BUT OF PEACE

My amazing wife and I, have spent decades working with crisis teens. Many of them were confused. I promise you this, if you had the things done to you, that were done to them, you'd be confused too.

1 Cor 14:32 NKJV
God is not the author of confusion, but of peace.

Many teens in treatment would have a medical & psychological team working with them.
Imagine this: (It's the 90's)
You are a very abused, desperate fourteen-year-old needing help. You are captured, locked in a hospital (sometimes strapped to your bed & sometimes locked in a

solitary padded room). You are then assigned a team of highly educated ungodly (sometimes atheist) adults, who are being paid very well - to "help" you. Two weeks into your treatment, the team can't help. Your file says: You are angry, violent, and refuse to follow simple instructions. You are disturbed and socially problematic. You are willing to harm yourself and others. The "team" is helpless. There's a storm inside of your mind and emotions that they can't calm. What does the team do?

The team agrees to sedate you heavily, and study you. The "team" shifts from involvement, to observation. Now, instead of helping you, they study you and how you respond to different sedatives for months on end.

In the mean-time, your file is stacked with speculative guesswork, and false assumptions. Our desperate teen is kept in a catatonic state under layers of prescription drugs. THE END???

NOPE

With a team of incredible people from church, we ran what the hospital called a "spirituality" program called Nite Life. We had the privilege of helping many of these kids simply by introducing them to Jesus. Love, prayer, Bible lessons, and hugs were what many of them needed. For well over two decades, we watched kids get saved and off all medications – very real miracles.

Mark 4:39 NKJV
"Then Jesus arose and rebuked the wind, and said to the sea, "Peace, be still!" And the wind ceased and there was a great calm."

The help we all need is for Jesus to calm our storms and give us peace. He heals and forgives.

Jesus loves us!!!

The wind and the sea obey Him. Nothing confusing about His help. IT IS MIRACULOUS!

Personally, after I accepted Christ as my savior, I had years of very good counseling. I needed to forgive & I needed forgiveness. I also needed to learn how to think right, act right, live right, talk right, and respond to life's challenges differently. I know God is not the author of confusion, but of peace because He calmed the storm inside of me.

My prayer:
Oh God, help me!
Lord please, whoever reads this - calm the storm inside of them!
Our help comes from You.
Thank You for washing away confusion and giving us peace!

Thank You for stepping into our messes and lifting us up. Thank You for the miracles You do because You love us. All praises and Glory and Honor, and Thanksgiving are due Your Precious Name.

In the name of The Lord Jesus Christ, Amen

Day 27

HELP MY UNBELIEF!

The disciples are arguing because none of them can cast a demon out of a boy. The boy is suffering and possessed, and his father feels completely helpless.
Jesus shows up, and finds out what's going on. The father begs Jesus to help if there's anything He can do...

Mark 9:22-24 NKJV

"If You can do anything, have compassion on us and help us." Jesus said to him, "If you can believe, all things are possible to him who believes." Immediately the father of the child cried out and said with tears, "Lord, I believe; help my unbelief!"

Discouragement can feel like quicksand. It pulls us down and suffocates us, making everything "seem" 100% hopeless. When we are hopeless, it's time for a miracle.

#1 Jesus said...
IF YOU CAN BELIEVE, ALL THINGS ARE POSSIBLE

He said this for us because we struggle with faith

#2 One of the most perfect responses any of us can offer: LORD I BELIEVE, HELP MY UNBELIEF!
This humble father aimed the tiny amount of faith he had in the perfect direction.

#3 JESUS PERFORMED A MIRACLE
Yes, to bless this family in the Bible, but also to help you and I believe right here and now two thousand years later

We're the ones who need help - Jesus said,
IF YOU CAN BELIEVE
God wants to help us overcome doubt and disbelief. Cry out with tears, and pull out the tiny amount of faith you have to work with, because it's priceless. Gather your

faith from underneath all the clutter life has dumped on you!
Bring all the faith you can find and aim it at Jesus.
Tell Him, Lord, I believe! Help my unbelief!!! Never stop believing, our help comes from the Lord.

My prayer:
Oh God, help me!
Lord, I believe, please help my unbelief! Please forgive me if there's anything unstable inside of me and help me to grow in my faith.
Thank You for the miracles You pour out every day that help us believe even more. Thank You for pouring out mercy and kindness when we struggle. Thank You for Your tender mercies that are new every morning.

In the name of The Lord Jesus Christ,
Amen

Day 28

MO BETTA

I grew up in New Orleans and we have special ways of saying things. Like, instead of just saying "better", we customize the words to express the idea at a new level, and say MO BETTA!
Well, I believe God has Mo Betta for you.

Ephesians 3:20-21 NKJV
"To Him who is able to do exceedingly abundantly above all that we ask or think, according to the power that works in us, to Him be glory in the church by Christ Jesus to all generations, forever and ever. Amen."

God loves me, and knows me, and He wants to do more for me than I can ask or imagine. When I pray, I often remind myself, that God has BETTER than I'm asking for – BETTER than I'm imagining while I'm asking. My sons and I joke about a line in Star Wars when Luke is trying to convince Han Solo to help him rescue Princess Leia. Luke tells Han, the reward would be "More wealth than you can imagine" and Han replies, "I don't know, I can imagine pretty much!"

When we read in Ephesians that God wants to do Exceedingly Abundantly above all we can ask or think, it blows my mind! God is saying He wants to do inconceivable things for us.

> **Lord, help me believe!**
> **Help me believe!**
> **Help me believe!**
> **God has Mo Betta for all of us!**

My prayer:
Oh God, help me!
Lord Your word tells us that Your ways are higher than ours, and that makes perfect sense. But I need Your help making room for things I can't imagine. Please help me

God to make room in my life for faith, and family, and career, and social blessing that I can't even imagine. Thank You Lord for wanting to give Your children such incredible levels of favor!!! Thank You Lord for being Wonderful!

In the name of The Lord Jesus Christ, Amen

Day 29

HELP ME TO HELP YOU HELP ME!

The last thing we want, is to stand before God and find out that when He wanted to help us, we got in His way...
God blessed King David enormously, but when David sinned against God, the Lord told David that He would have given him "much more".

II Samuel 12:7-8 NKJV
"I anointed you king over Israel, and I delivered you from the hand of Saul. I gave you your master's house and your master's wives into your keeping, and gave you the house of Israel and Judah. **And if that had been too little, I also would have given you much more!**"

Right in the middle of his shortcomings, God tells David that He wanted to bless him even more than He already had. That's

like cheating to win the super-bowl and getting DQ'd -
only to find out afterwards that God was already planning to give you the win. That is disappointing disappointment.
I don't want God to tell me what could have been. Let's turn away from terrible ideas, and run from foolishness! Let's believe God for the help we need to get there with faith and integrity.
Let's find out what God has in store for us, instead of missing it, or messing everything up!

This is why I called todays devotion...
HELP ME TO HELP YOU HELP ME!

We want to help God help us! We don't want to get in the way of Him helping us, right?

My prayer:
Oh God, help me!
Lord, help me to get out of Your way!
But help me to always do my part. Deliver me from evil, and help me to walk uprightly.
Help me to let You lead and call the shots. Help me to back off and not push or force my own agendas. Let Your will be done on earth as it is in Heaven. Thank You Lord, cause now I know, You want to do MUCH MORE for me than I am actually aware of. Help me understand that.
Thank You for patiently waiting for me to figure things out. Your faithfulness is such an amazing blessing. And thank You for lovingly leading me into the help You know I need!

In the name of The Lord Jesus Christ,
Amen

Day 30

NAY SAYERS

Maybe you don't know this, but there are people who will look you in the face and tell you, "God can't, God won't, and God doesn't".

It's true and terrible; they have chosen not to believe, and their message is one of disbelief.
There are world-wide Christian denominations that state in their doctrine, that God doesn't speak to people and that He doesn't do miracles anymore. They say those days have passed.
Lemme tell you something, I don't want *those* people visiting me in the hospital!

Romans 3:3-4 NKJV
"For what if some did not believe? Will their unbelief make the faithfulness of God without effect? Certainly not! Indeed, let

God be true but every man a liar. As it is written: "That You may be justified in Your words, and may overcome when You are judged."

If I'm gonna go down, I'm going down believing God's Word.
Let God's Word tell you what is and isn't possible.
Let God's Word tell you what God will and will not do.
Let God's Word be the foundation of everything you believe as a Christian.

I've had ministers tell me...
"God doesn't do that"

But God did do that.

I've had people tell me "that's off" only to find IT WAS DEAD ON

My wife and I have believed for miracles against everything natural and economically possible - and God has done multiple miracles for us.

I have had God speak to me clearly on many different occasions, and it changed the course of my life, my education, my career, our family, our finances, everything!

Don't ever tell someone that God can't - and at the same time, don't let others tell YOU God can't.
Let God be true and every man a liar

My prayer:
Oh God, help me!
Lord, You are so good and there's no one like You!
Help me to welcome Your supernatural help into EVERY part of my life and family.
Help me to be a stable, wise, experienced, faith filled Christian that spreads faith!
Help me never to hinder someone else's faith.

Help me to encourage others to put all their hope and trust in You! Help me more, show me more, teach me more! You are my Rock and this world is sinking sand. Thank You for rescuing me from a life without miracles! Thank You for helping me navigate troubled waters.
Thank You for being true to Your Word!

In the name of The Lord Jesus Christ, Amen

LAGNIAPPE

(Lan-yap): A little extra for free

LAGNIAPPE 1

DON'T GET HELP FROM THE WRONG SOURCES, AND DON'T GET SNARKY

This is definitely a thread in the tapestry of this devotional. I know, on any given day, we can be sailing along, singing a song, and what "appears" to be good help is available. We can all jump into things without looking, or without asking. Inquire of God, ask. Pray about everything. And don't devalue the treasure of seeking help from God.

1 Thess 5:17 NKJV
PRAY WITHOUT CEASING

God told King Amaziah not to accept help from any of the children of Ephraim, but

Amaziah had already agreed to let Ephraim help him. So, in order to obey God, Amaziah had to cancel his previous agreement with the children of Ephraim. This upset them, but it also saved Amaziah's life and his army.
II Chronicles 25:8 NKJV
"But if you go, be gone! Be strong in battle! Even so, God shall make you fall before the enemy; for God has power to help and to overthrow."

God has the power to help or to overthrow, so don't form alliances with people, or businesses, or organizations - whatever, without His blessing.
And if you already have, and God says don't. Then, take your losses and withdraw. God is trying to help you.

But (like an infomercial) wait, there's more! God helped King Amaziah obtain a great victory after canceling his agreement with Ephraim.

But guess what Amaziah did next? After defeating the Edomites, Amaziah took their idols from their temple and set up a place for them in his palace. SAY WHAT?

II Chronicles 25:14 NKJV
"After Amaziah came from the slaughter of the Edomites, that he brought the gods of the people of Seir, set them up to be his gods, and bowed down before them and burned incense to them." Well, this bothered God, so God sent a prophet to offer some life-saving advice to Amaziah.

II Chronicles 25:15-16 NKJV
The anger of the Lord was aroused against Amaziah, and He sent him a prophet who said to him, "Why have you sought the gods of the people, which could not rescue their own people from your hand?" So it was, as he talked with him, that the king said to him, "Have we made you the king's counselor? Cease! Why should you be

killed?" Then the prophet ceased, and said, "I know that God has determined to destroy you, because you have done this and have not heeded my advice."

So even when there was some hope left for Amaziah - he got snarky and threatened to kill the man of God. One measly victory and Amaziah was
un-help-able. Remember, it was God that gave him that victory.

My prayer:
Oh God, help me!
Lord I always want to accept Your help!
Please help me never to be so full of myself that I can't even comprehend Your mercy and kindness and generosity.
Help me to be aware of things lurking in my flesh that can bring destruction. And help me to rid myself of prideful insanity!

Thank You Lord for Your Word and the precious stories that can save my life. Thank You for showing me how You send help and advice. Thank You for letting me see that Your heart is to help. I love and need You every day.

In the name of The Lord Jesus Christ, Amen

LAGNIAPPE 2

OUR HERITAGE

Our fore-fathers of the faith all asked God for help. At one point King Darius made it illegal to pray, unless it was to him. Ridiculous right? But His officials had actually tricked him so they could kill Daniel.
Now all they had to do was follow Daniel to see when he would break the law. If anyone broke the King's prayer law, they would be fed to the lions.

Daniel 6:11 NLT
Then the officials went to Daniel's house and found him praying and asking for God's help.

It's a good thing he asked God for help! Daniel was arrested and thrown in the lion's den. But God shut the mouths of the lions. The bad people who tricked the king and set Daniel up were fed to the lions instead.

Ask God for help no matter what.

Things I personally pray on a regular basis:
- Help me to forgive
- Help me to keep forgiving
- Help me to learn & grow
- Help me to think right
- Help me to put You first and keep You first in everything
- Help me to know when I'm slacking
- Help me never to be flaky
- Help me to be patient
- Help me not to compare myself to others
- Help me to trust You and not my feelings
- Help me to lead others to Christ
- Help me to see trouble and avoid it

My prayer:
OH GOD, THANK YOU FOR HELPING ME!
Lord, please use all these teachings to move me forward and experience greater success in You. Help me to remember, every day, to call on You no matter what! Lord, help me to share Your loving kindness with everyone I come in contact with.

In the name of The Lord Jesus Christ,
Amen

Made in the USA
Columbia, SC
12 March 2024